Parenting with a Purpose

Sara,

May God Bless you and
your Family always!

Ricardo Willie
June 26, 16

Parenting with a Purpose

Equipping Kids To Succeed in Life

Your children will mirror what you do, they will mirror who you are. Make sure your reflection is one worth manifesting into the future.

Ricardo Miller, Sr.

Rev. date: 01/11/2016

To order additional copies of this book, contact:
Xlibris
1-888-795-4274
www.Xlibris.com
Orders@Xlibris.com
650259

CONTENTS

PURPOSE in SUPPORT

Dedication

To each of you, who have helped propel me into my PURPOSE...

My Father God, whose eyes I follow as they closely watch His children grow and daily shows me more of His heart.

His Son Jesus, who in obedience walked *purposefully*, determined to do what He was born to do – set mankind free.

The Holy Spirit, for His patience and encouragement as I collaborate with Him in the commission to *"Raise the Standard in Children's Ministry."*

Dearest Isha, my loving wife and mother of my son: for all your support, covering, and partnership with me in impacting this generation with the kingdom message and in raising our son to be an influential young man and leader.

Bishop Dean Wells, whose transgenerational anointing I have observed with admiration for years, and reflects in the theme of this book. Apostle Raymond Wells, who has covered me as a father in the faith since I gave my life to Christ at the age of 18. My Senior Pastor, Danny Wegman – a man who has put his hand to the plow, faithfully serving and covering the same congregation for more than 30 years; his has been an incredible example that I am greatly proud to follow.

My friends in ministry, Pastor Dominick Antonino, Apostle George Jobe, Pastor Mario Ramos, Pastor Franco Charles, Dr. Terran Dames, Pastor Kelly James, Pastor Lawrence Otto, and my Children's Ministry brothers and sisters who faithfully serve kids all around the world.

My mother Eunice, who diligently continues in her vigorous concern for her children through her prayers for our family, and directing the Father's blessings from generation to generation.

PURPOSE in Parenting

Children are the living messages we send to a time we will not see.

PARENTING.

Raising children can be exhausting, complicated, frustrating, unexpected and above all else…neverending.

Whew!

But you know what? I'm divinely convinced that in spite of every emotion that purchases a ticket aboard the *Parental Express*, there's no task on earth quite as rewarding as raising a child.

Listen, parenting is the biggest job we will ever attempt to master in life. And just like any corporate position, we can find ourselves overworked, overwhelmed and underpaid – with incentives showing themselves few and far between. So, pretty normal for the most part, right? But unlike that fresh position we may have just been blessed with on our jobs, brand new parents just don't have the luxury of having paid training, a step by step manual outlining mandatory Standard Operating Procedures, or an overseer to gently guide us through the exciting ride we are about to navigate.

Instead, this cute little bundle of joy equipped with ten fingers and toes to match comes crashing into their lives demanding attention – and for whatever reason, babies refuse to wait out the 90 day probationary period as Mom and Dad hoped for.

Go figure.

Most parents come armed with a thousand questions that they just pray someone – anyone, will be able to answer to relieve their impending anxiety. The awesome thing is, when kids respond to those unasked inquires with an impromptu hug, a smile stretching from one side of Texas to the other, or just a look in their eyes that says "I love you", sometimes those small gestures hold the answers parents are looking for. And because a child's unconditional affection can often be reward enough, parents can rest a bit easier knowing that they may not always get it right, may not have all the answers, but at least they are on the right track in their journey.

So here's why *Parenting With a Purpose* is in *your* hands. *PWAP* is a cohesive collection of questions and answers I have complied to spiritually push you as a purpose driven parent into the divine role God has called you to. I want to ignite your imagination to pull out the creative thoughts, fiery opinions, and original ideas resting inside every child. You answer each of my challenges honestly, and you can be assured that by the end of *Parenting With a Purpose*, you will have better insight regarding the plan God has for your child and how you can help propel them into their destiny.

"When a child is not allowed to develop their passion, they begin to feel ripped off…that's how we end up with a bunch of thirty-something's who hate going to their jobs." ~ Ricardo Miller, Sr.

PURPOSE in Improving Parental Skills

Behind every child who believes in himself are parents who believed first.

You want to purposely be a successful parent?

Successful parenting requires being strategic and intentional about every step you take to get the results you want. Please believe that a *motivated* child can look to the bleachers during the game and find a *motivated* parent right there cheering them on loud and unashamed!

In other words – it ain't gonna be easy, my friends!

I've seen it before and it never fails: if the parent does nothing, the child does even less. Say for instance, you desire to shed a few extra pounds that are giving you the blues. The unwelcome weight won't magically melt or drop off. You've got to construct an eating plan, schedule time in the gym, and generally reorganize your lifestyle before you will be satisfied by tangible results your own eyes can see and kiss the former you good-bye.

Well, the same principle applies when parents expect little Timmy to do his best in school and eventually work his way up through higher education. Timmy needs to witness Mom and Dad honing their child-rearing skill set by making wise decisions and putting forth their best efforts to provide a better life for him. But if Mom and Dad sleep all day and leave Timmy to be raised by social media, 52-inch flatscreens playing their favorite shows and video games that tend to tip on the opposite side of moral (kids don't even like to go outdoors these days, geesh) then what behavior do you think Timmy will mimic?

Iron sharpens iron. It's not a cliché, nor a cute quote for us to haphazardly sling around to color our conversations. It's the absolute Biblical truth (Proverbs 27:17). Parenting just isn't easy. We have to be *sharpened* in order to be successful.

It is my sincere prayer that this manual help sharpen the skills living on the inside of you!

Let's start with seven practical tips to help you sharpen your parental skill set.

1- Doing the right things.

Not my child! Oh really, now? No matter how much we wholeheartedly want to believe our children will consistently behave outside the view of those eyes we have planted in the back of our heads, we know that won't always be the case. However, we can increase the likelihood of them doing the right things by modeling what good behavior looks like for them. Controversial situations, arguments, disagreements - how we respond and react to adversity in front of them speaks volumes to our children. The old saying goes: if you want to know how someone really feels about you...ask their kids! Effective parenting means sometimes using a filter for our emotions. Not all behavior is hereditary; much of it is learned. (*"She's just like her mother!" "He's just like his father!"*) Doing the right thing isn't always easy, but it is necessary. Ephesians 6:4 "Fathers do not exasperate your children; instead bring them up in the training and instruction if the Lord." You do the right thing, and chances are good your children will, too.

2- Doing the right things right

Parents aren't always right. But we like to think we are.

So when I say *do the right things right*, it's not about simply following the instructions like you'll find on the back box when you're baking a cake. If you take all the ingredients, dump them into a bowl and pop the mixture into the oven without taking the time to carefully consult the instructions, your dessert is going to come out dry, unsavory and unappealing! Some rules must be followed the right way.

I'm a serious health and fitness advocate. I don't just rock the clothes or pose on some fancy equipment; I consistently work out at the gym at least three or four times a week. It's my lifestyle.

For me, consistency is key in reaching my fitness goals. Now I don't have any specific weight I'm trying to achieve, but simply maintaining a good healthy balance in my body is important to me. I admit, I have used a personal trainer to help me out before, and here's a little revelation I picked up from that experience:

When the trainer instructed me to do squats, I did the right thing, and completed them. But catch this – when I first tried, although I had good intentions, I didn't do the exercise *right*, so I didn't see any results. Go figure. But once I tried again, executing the squats according to the proper form and posture that I was initially taught, I got the results I wanted… because I did the right thing *right*.

I've met so many parents who told me, *"But Ricardo I am doing that."* However, once we sat down and assessed their activities together, we discovered that they made a good attempt in doing the right thing, but fell short of actually doing it *right*. For example, you can draw up an impeccable, colorful and even artsy chart outlining chores that your kiddo is responsible for completing. However, if you fail to post the chart in a visible place and never follow up to make sure the chores are done, not only have you wasted good ink and paper, now you didn't do the right thing – *right*. Consequently, the chores haven't been done and you're left huffing, puffing and wanting to blow the house down. Make sense?

1ˢᵗ Timothy 3:4 "He must manage his own family well and see that his children obey him, and he must do so In a manner worthy of full respect." Make every effort to do the right things right, and the harmony in your home will sing just a bit louder.

3- Doing the right things better

Dear parent - you have to be committed to learning how you can improve on what you are doing right that can still be done *better*. Growth is necessary for continual success in anything, right? Businesses thrive more as they evolve through new technological systems and marketing initiatives. Teachers often go back to school themselves to keep up with the ever-changing educational system. Even entertainers find great longevity by constantly reinventing themselves as they grow in such an unpredictable industry. Two key words to make note of here are *better* and *learning*. You can't go wrong when you are committed to learning and becoming better as a parent. Ecclesiastes 9:10 says, "*Whatever your hand finds to do, do it with all of your might, for in the realm of the dead, where you are going there is neither working nor planning nor knowledge nor wisdom.*" Wisdom tells us that there's always room for improvement. Especially when it comes to taking care of a child.

4- Doing what other people are doing

Earlier, I mentioned that kids tend to mimic their parent's behavior. Well, Mom/Dad - don't you be afraid to mimic the systems of other parents whose track records are tried, true and tangibly successful! Remember, someone is succeeding where you are failing. So don't be too proud to ask for help. No one knows it all, but it never hurts to seek wise counsel. Ask for help. School counselors, pastors, coaches, even other parents are here to help. Mathew 7:7 says "Ask and it shall be given, seek and you will find, knock and the door will be opened." Get your questions ready and go for it, my friends!

5- Doing away with things.

It's not always hard to say goodbye. In life, there are things working against your success as a parent, so they have to go. That could mean making a commitment to move from a certain neighborhood, shutting down the T.V. for a while, cutting off some friends, maybe even taking away some unearned privileges from your child. If it's not helping and you know it's affecting your relationship with your child, then it could be something that needs to go. Mathew 5:30 says it best: "If your right hand causes you to stumble, cut it off and throw it away. It is better for you to lose one part of your body than for your whole body to go into hell." Cut the strings and let it go!

6- Doing things no one else is doing.

It's time to get creative and be different! Just because all the other Moms and Dads are doing it, does not make it a right fit for your family.

Growing up in Nassau, there was a family of kids on the block whose parents were raising them totally different than the rest of us. We'd hang out in the streets, but these kids had to stay in the house. We'd jump on our bikes and zip through the neighborhood, but they could only go so far and had a strict curfew! And when we got to hang out after school, guess who had to get home as soon as the last bell rang? You guessed it.

As a kid, we thought the rules those kids' folks made them follow were pretty whack. I mean, where was all the fun for Pete's sake? But I found out later that while my friends' lives didn't turn out perfect, they got in a lot less trouble than many of the other kids who ran freely. It might be hard to stand out amongst the crowd, but it is possible with God's help. Whether your child is growing up in a challenging neighborhood or a prestigious one, it's okay – even *great*, to be different. Stand your ground. Luke 18:27 "*Then Jesus replied, 'What is impossible with man is possible with God.'*"

Doing things like no one else is doing keeps people (and your children) alert, intrigued, and always ready to see what's next.

7- Doing things, no else has done.

Consider this: As a parent, God may be calling you to defy the odds and do what no one else has done in parenting. Yes, *YOU*! That means, for the sake of your kids and your heritage, sometimes you have to separate yourself and your family. Folk may talk about you. Let them talk. Folk may laugh. Let them laugh. Folk may not understand what you are doing; keep them guessing! If the environment you are subjecting your children to is not provoking them to become the best they can be, then change your environment and do something different. Philippians 4:13 says "*I can do all things through Christ who strengthens me.*"

You have the strength to do it. God's given you the power to do it. Now all you have to do is walk boldly in the skin that He's covered you in and be the innovator that you are destined to be.

PURPOSE in the Age We Live in

The best job in the world is being a parent!

I mean, we get to train, inspire, and have the ultimate reward of watching our children grow up. But it's easy to get bogged down wearing so many hats that our dream job can get to be a bit complicated. We may find ourselves slacking when it comes to recognizing and adapting to the ideals of raising children in this generation – and that my friend, is when our journey can get a bit sticky.

Kids right now, all over the nation, are faced with more than I ever could have imagined as a child. And as much as we may try to instill faith in them, let's face it – this is a faithless generation!

Christian children have the odds stacked against them in school, community organizations, and most of the places they frequent. Eventually, many of them end up hiding their true beliefs and convictions just for the sake of fitting in.

Can you believe that in a large majority of audiences I speak to, very few students raise their hand when I ask if they pray before having lunch at school? Why do you think that is? It's as if the kids believe the Savior they praised on Sunday doesn't care whether they own Him on Monday!

It's our duty to drive the scriptures home in our children's hearts, so they have the power to stand on their faith in any situation. Let's keep reiterating to them that Matthew 10:33 pertains to them too: "...*but whoever denies me before men, I also will deny before my Father who is in heaven.*"

We have to take an honest look at today's child and equip them with the resources they need as believers to walk, talk and live the Word of God. We're not asking them to preach...just helping them to stand firm in their beliefs. Keep providing them with the foundation, and I guarantee they'll keep constructing the remainder of the building.

"*It's easier to build strong children, than repair broken men.*" (Frederick Douglass).

PURPOSE in Parental Involvement

"There are very few things wrong with our schools that raising the quality of parenting would not solve."

One of my favorite times of the year is when our children's ministry team hosts our annul lock-in. Eight years strong, the kids always have crazy fun at this event: staying up all night, playing games, all the food they can pig out on, watching movies, clowning around in bounce houses and hanging with their friends...a mere 12 hours of pure bliss! It's the rave of the church and I guess it's safe to say, the annual event is always a huge WIN for our children's department!

Now here's the rest of the story —

During the most recent lock-in, I initially believed a twist our team added in would be a sure fire success. We offered a FREE *"Parenting With a Purpose"* seminar for the first hour of the lock-in. The only requirement parents had was to register, attend the session and then be kid-free for the rest of the night. A perfect win-win, right? At least it *sounded* that way. Do you know that no one even signed up to attend? Not one parent showed up for the workshop.

I couldn't believe it! Completely baffled...flabbergasted. I mean, this was a free opportunity for parents to come and get some of that iron sharpening I discussed earlier. But had

I considered the climate in our school system and lack of parental involvement in it, I wouldn't have been too surprised.

Hey, if we want to initiate change in our children's lives and culture, parents have to be involved in *every* aspect of their development. Including *education*. Parents are often the single biggest missing component in our schools. It's not lack of money, teachers, resources or equipment. It's Mom and Dad being involved.

Mom/Dad, if you're going to fulfill your purpose, resist the urge to dismiss those notices for parent/teacher conferences at school or church. Get up and GO! Honestly, parents who carve out the extra time to attend these meetings have successful children who go beyond expectations. You will be hard pressed to identify a parent of a child who is doing poorly at one of these meetings; When parents show they care, kids will find a way to make the most of educational opportunities and spiritual development.

Now the kids may not want me to reveal this little secret to you guys, but folder and backpack checks produce a wealth of information! Almost everything you need to know about your child's home away from home is in the bag. Yes, it's the job of the school teacher/children's ministry worker to teach and minister to your child; however, it's the job of the parent to enforce what the teachers teach. So check it out. Without guilt.

Do not be afraid to take control and conduct the train transporting your child to their destiny. Your involvement now, will lead to their GRATITUDE later.

PURPOSE in Encouraging Your Child

Although some popular gospel music may offer a word to the contrary, it's not a child's purpose to encourage themselves!

It's simple: a child looks to adults for approval, but they crave *encouragement* from their parents. Did you know that encouragement should unconditionally be standard language from parent to child from birth? Here's why: positive affirmation keeps kids wanting to do the right thing simply because they see their folks are pleased. Believe it or not – that's often reward enough for them. A child encouraged by their parents is motivated to be a happy, productive child in society.

The tongue is most definitely sharper than a two-edged sword. Words do hurt, but they can also heal. Using affirming words with our children, gives them confidence and builds self-assurance; hey, they even start *believing* that they are "good enough!" Uplifting statements like *"You can do it"* or *"Thank you for giving your best"* can go a long way when life's pressures begin to mount. And whether we know it or not, our children *do* face pressure. When kids believe they are not quite measuring up to the standards good old Mom and Dad set (either from peers at school or at home), the pressure is on!

Encouragement comes easier when we focus on wı kids are doing right. For example - what are his/her stren̰ Organizing? Public speaking? Drawing? Fearlessness? ̤et them know you see how good they are these things and it will build a world of self-esteem!

When a child regularly hears words of encouragement, they don't dismiss it as fluff; they believe it inside. Everyday life is clouded with negativity outside of our homes; children are bombarded with images and influences that want to shape their character, morality, thoughts and behavior. (And not all of it is pretty). As the primary voice of influence in their lives, parents must aim to create a positive, God-centered image for our kids.

Kick things off by affirming your child is created in God's image and He is good! What God places within us is good – so don't call your child otherwise. (*"He is so bad!"*)

Even when our children fail or miss the mark, there is still a place for encouragement. Let them know they can get back up and try again. Now we don't want shoddy work, but it's still important not to kill the spirit of the child by speaking down to them.

"Do not let any unwholesome talk come out of your mouths, but only what is helpful for building others up, according to their needs, that it may benefit those who listen." - (Eph. 4:29)

Speak life!

PURPOSE POINTS

Have you taught your children that some friends are so perfect for us that they are put into the category of angels? We know that they could only have been sent by God.

_____

When life seems dark and dreary and no hope can be seen, the power of friendship is there to help us remain strong against adversity.

_____

When a friend starts taking away from your happiness and creating more stress, it could be a sign you need to extinguish the relationship.

PURPOSE in "NO"

Listen, sometimes parents are so busy trying to befriend their kids – they forgo RAISING them with correction.

Children need discipline, boundaries, rules…and it's the PURPOSE of the parents to enforce them. That means we have to be intentionally bold and firm about setting guidelines. There's a single word that will shape and mold the direction our kids' lives more profoundly than any material thing we can ever give them. And that's the gift of "NO." Telling our kids *NO* gives them guidance, sets up social limitations, and helps them understand everything in life does not come delivered with a fancy bow and seal of approval.

"Dad, can I play my Xbox?" "Mom, can I go over to Chris' this weekend"? Questions, questions, questions – well, no better place than here to start teaching our children to accept *NO* for an answer. Sometimes, it's important to realize that we have to say it *just because*. There is power in *NO* and we don't always have to justify why we said it. Not trying to be mean or unjust, but kids need to be coached into understanding rejection as a part of life.

Without the ability to *accept* *NO* as an answer, our little ones grow up believing all things must go in their favor. (i.e, *spoiled*). Then when they're told *NO* at school or by friends, our kids may not know how to process rejection. (*Note – we want to keep our kids from bullying teachers/ministry workers into having their own way; it starts at home*). Thinking back on my own upbringing, I firmly believe *NO* actually helps boost kid's ability to make sound choices and decisions.

The Bible says, "Train up a child in the way they should go and when they are older they will not depart from it." (Proverbs 22:6). Watch this - knowing how to choose to *indulge in* or *reject* certain behaviors is a part of training kids to accept *NO*.

As children grow older and their personality develops, *NO* should be a common part of their *home* training. That means attitude is everything. It's critical that when parents say *NO*, the child accepts it without a change in demeanor or mood. A positive attitude confirms the child has heard the response, accepts it and moves on.

A single *NO* can mean one less call from the school about bullying (either as the victim or the agitator), failed tests or an urgent need for an attitude adjustment - because the child has been properly trained up.

PURPOSE POINTS

Do you listen not only to what is being said,
but to the message behind the words?

Have you taught your children that if you can obtain
it overnight, you can lose it just as quickly?

Have you taught your children to limit their exposure to
negative circumstances and, if possible, make the best of it?

PURPOSE in Remaining Calm

My fellow parents, if there's one thing I've learned on my own journey as a parent and children's ministry leader is that teaching children to accept *No* is only the beginning... they have to learn to control their *emotions* as well.

The disciple Peter was quick to cut off an ear, but if we try that guerilla tactic when we don't get our way in today's society, it's pretty safe to say we'll be looking at more than a quick *time out* in a corner when the dust settles, right? Let's face it: when you're mad, you're mad - but parental duties include teaching our kids that they can't scream and bark at every situation beyond their control. Look at this way – parents with PURPOSE have the unique opportunity to be the illustration of composure under tough circumstances that our children need to see for themselves. How, you ask? Everybody just remain...*calm.*

Matthew 5:45 informs us that "...he lets rain fall on the just and the unjust." By teaching our children the art of staying calm, not only are we helping them stay out of trouble, they're getting equipped with a skill they'll be appreciative of as they navigate through life's frustrations.

Friends, we may have faith and follow Christ, but that doesn't mean we can blink our eyes and shoo trouble away just because we believe. How we handle catching curve balls in the game not only determines the final score, but also reflects who we are in Christ. Ever see an athlete behave like a poor sport? Chances are they haven't been trained to accept bad calls or defeat in peace.

Children have to learn as early as possible that looking like Christ means peacefully letting His light shine even when they feel cheated, disappointed or let down.

So what does learning to stay calm look like?

Well for one thing, it's issuing a cease-and-desist to the instinctive desire to throw a good old fashioned temper tantrum. If a young child can do that, it's a sure sign they're learning to control their emotions.

If parents lead by example, children are more likely to emulate their folk's unfazed reaction when a frustrating *opportunity* presents itself. Showing kids the appropriate reaction versus just telling them goes a long way. For parents, that means don't be aggressive and save the drama; correct the situation in love and your child will learn to do the same.

No matter what part of the world you are from, there's a universal situation in everybody's childhood that will make a kid mad enough to want to go upside somebody's head: Somebody takes their toy without permission. Oh, that's almost like trying to snatch a T-bone steak away from a pitbull! Here's a great opportunity to instill calm in children, especially before a fight breaks out. The child can either learn to share or politely ask for the toy to be returned. Either way, parents have to demonstrate these reactions for them first.

Proverbs 25:11 *"Like apples of gold in settings of silver is a word spoken in right circumstance."* Look, adversity is notorious for poor timing. It never shows up at a convenient time, does it? Well for children (and even many adults) learning how to manage emotions when adversity unexpectedly checks in for a visit takes practice. Teach your children how to think ahead and consider the outcome before responding to a tense situation.

It's never too late to start teaching this principle. Whether 5 or 15, your child can learn how to manage his or her emotions. Below, I'm giving you five methods to practice keeping calm that will help you and your child keep from blowing up:

1. Take a deep breath.
2. Tell yourself to "Be calm" or count to ten.
3. Share your feelings and consider why you feel this way.
4. Tell someone you trust what is bothering you.
5. Try solving the situation that made you upset.

Print these tips out and keep them nearby. You may not need to reference them today, but believe me…the opportunity for you to put them into play may come sooner than you think. You'll be glad you did.

PURPOSE in Asking for Help

In ministry, I've had a blast operating in my PURPOSE - reaching thousands of kids, all different, unique and awesome in their own way! Yet, they have one major trait in common – they want to be *independent*.

Kids need to prove they are growing up by doing everything for themselves. Alright my friend, don't be alarmed! Independence is beneficial for the healthy development of your child. However, as excited as they are to show Mom and Dad what they learned how to do on their own - it's critical that children also realize that asking for help is important, too. Parents have to teach kids how and when to ask for help.

Let me pause real quick to make one thing clear: there is a difference between *asking* and *demanding*. No one owes our children anything, so we have to teach them to differentiate between the two. Then after we teach them *how* to ask, we have to advise them it's up to folk to choose whether they want to help or not - and kids should appreciate whatever response they get. (Independence requires maturity).

If we don't start teaching them while they are young, many children become adults who don't know how to properly ask for help. (*"Please"* and *"Thank you"* go a long way…but use of both has to be taught). It amazes me how many adults don't know how to properly ask for help. Don't let this trend sneak into *your* home; start now in guiding your child on how to ask for help by:

1. Deciding if they can easily accomplish the task without help.
2. Finding the best person skilled enough to help with the task.
3. Clearly articulating what they need from the individual they are asking help from.
4. Asking pleasantly and politely.
5. Thanking the person for helping them.

Sometimes, people become frustrated and even get mad when they can't figure something out. Getting help is often the best way to solve problems we can't figure out on our own. Learning in childhood that asking for help before we reach the breaking point will yield more successes than failures.

Now, requesting assistance in a pleasant manner makes it more likely that someone will want to do so. (*I learned this the hard way*). Asking someone who has more experience, or has had more success with a similar problem to step in, is a way to learn how to solve it the next time. I really wish I had started this practice early on in my children's ministry career.

No matter how the situation ends, good etiquette is always in order. Let's teach our offspring to follow assistance up with appreciation. Once they've mastered the art of "asking," help the kids exercise the good manners of saying *"Thank you!"*

PURPOSE POINTS

The only possibility of your success in parenting or
any area is in knowing God called you to do it.

As a parent, be married to principles but not to methods.

PURPOSE in Asking Permission

"Can I?" "May I?" Parents – **coming from both sides of the coin (formerly as a child and now as a parent), I can safely confirm that *kids are inherently programmed to deliver one of these questions at least a minimum of five times on a daily basis!***

No worries, though. The same way we teach our kids to ask for *help*, they've got to learn how to ask for *permission*, yes? Parents with PURPOSE teach their children proper ways to ask for permission leading to getting the positive results they are looking for. This *"gimmie"* mindset like the world owes us something can change the entire outcome we anticipated, then here we go again trying to make sure our kids know how to accept *No* with grace and humility like we taught them earlier. Trust me – you do not want that old *whoa is me* song on repeat in your house!

Did you know five is the number of grace? Well grab your highlighter, because here are five ways to teach your child to *gracefully* ask permission and accept the outcome with humility:

1. Look at the other person.
2. Be specific and articulate when asking permission; the other person should know exactly what is being requested.

3. Be sure to ask rather than demand. *"May I please ...?"*
4. Give reasons if necessary.
5. Accept the decision without change in attitude.

Whether it's an activity they want to participate in, or use of something that another person is responsible for, kids have to ask first, right? Does your child just grab a slice of cake off the pan before dinner is even served without asking you first, Mom and Dad? Chances of that are highly unlikely – they may find themselves sent to their rooms with no dinner, dessert, television, phone or electronic devices at all simply for overstepping their boundaries.

Many young people haven't been taught to ask permission first, and then find themselves in trouble with authority figures. It's not cute. Asking permission shows respect for others and increases the probability that the request will be granted. That sweet tooth little Suzie wanted has more of a shot to be satisfied with that slice of cake she desired *IF* she asks her folks permission first...to which they may respond "Sure, after dinner sweetie." After her plate is cleaned, she already has gotten permission and it's on!

Wisdom is children asking permission no matter what the situation is. Sometimes, they won't get what they want, but it's the right thing to do.

PURPOSE-Filled Communication

If nothing else in the world relies on PURPOSE... communication sure does! PURPOSE is the protagonist of communication; without it, there's no point.

Poor communication is frowned upon, but it's not always properly taught. Friends, we are in a technology takeover! These days, kids would rather converse through keyboards and touch screens rather than open up their mouths and speak. I suspect that's because they haven't quite mastered the art of proper communication. Honestly, it's kind of painful to witness. How can an adult comfortably interview for a new job, when they never learned to speak as a child? So you see why it's critically important to teach children how to communicate face to face with others.

If they're going to ask for help, if they're going to ask for permission, kids have to learn to effectively communicate their needs and desires first. How, you say? I'm so glad you have all the right questions, Friend! Here's five (grace) tips I've compiled to jump start your child on the path to effective communication:

1. Give more than a "Yes" or "No" response to any question asked of them in complete sentences. This

type of answer usually does not give the other person enough information to keep the conversation going. Since our son was young, we've always taught him to be very descriptive in his responses and to think before he answers. It takes practice, but with consistent use this tactic becomes second nature.

2. Ask questions. Start or add to conversations by asking questions, talking about new or exciting events or asking the other person's opinion can lead to bonding and building lasting friendships or relationships.

3. Use appropriate grammar. One of the biggest pet peeves my wife has is using improper grammar. Properly articulating words and pronunciation shows you have the intellect to talk with anyone. There's nothing wrong with slang, but using it in the appropriate setting is paramount.

4. Look the other person in the eye. Even though in other cultures this can be seen as having a lack of respect, it's normal in Western culture. As your child develops, distinguish this communication technique so they will know when and how to use it.

5. Avoid negative conversations. Talking about past trouble they were in, talking negatively about others or making other derogatory statements leaves a bad impression.

Life can tend to be awkward enough on its own. People feel more comfortable with us when we know how to speak to them. It may seem small, but things like including the other person's ideas in the conversation helps validate what they are saying, and they can tell we are actually listening. Growing up in the Bahamas, I never practiced this behavior; these days as a children's ministry leader, I do. Now I appreciate and understand the importance of proper communication, and so do the people I am talking to.

It's never too early to ditch the baby talk and teach our children how to communicate with ease.

PURPOSE POINTS

Your goals are the road map which guide you and show you what is possible for your life. Are you working your goals?

What does "success" for your family look like? What is the predetermined goal that you set for your family and children?

Do your children know that they can come to you and admit their mistakes...knowing that you are "faithful and just to forgive them"?

PURPOSE-Filled Compliments

Who doesn't crack a smile when they receive a compliment?

It feels like someone just blessed us with a gift, doesn't it? The first compliment I received as a teenager working with the children in the neighborhood surrounding our church propelled me into my PURPOSE of becoming a children's ministry specialist!

Back then, a number of the parents, church leaders and adult workers overseeing our ministry program saw something special in the way I was reaching the kids; they complimented me on the program's success due to my efforts, and it changed my life! Now, I see the power of *giving* compliments and teaching children how to compliment *others* for themselves.

Compliments do not hurt. They build! We never know how it can make someone's day to receive a compliment, especially if that person is discouraged. Now I really like the tips I'm listing for you below, because it teaches our kids that they are blessed to be a blessing to others! Here are four ways to teach our kids to give the gift of a compliment:

1. Whether it's that awesome outfit they're rocking, the new fabulous hairstyle, upbeat personality, the good grade they earned on the toughest assignment, have

your child sincerely consider what they like about the person that is appropriate to compliment.

2. After deciding what they would like to compliment, tell the person about it!

3. Have you ever heard someone say, "*Your hair looks nice...but it would look better like this?*" Teach them to avoid following up compliments with negative statements; it minimizes the nice things they've said.

4. If the person says "*Thanks,*" the child should respond with "*You're welcome*" in return. And even if the person doesn't say thanks, teach your child not to allow that to hinder them from giving compliments in the future.

In children's ministry, we compliment, compliment, compliment – it inspires our kids to come out of their shells, get involved and give more of their very best! They get excited and learn that extending compliments shows that we notice the accomplishments of others. After all, kids like hearing nice things about themselves. It helps build positive esteem, which in the long run is healthy and the ability to say something nice about others reflects the confidence we have in ourselves!

PURPOSE in Building Self-Esteem

Big head. Big foot. Big nose. Growing up, I was called all of these things, and my self-esteem paid the price for it. Believe it or not, at one time in my life, I was even called "shorty" too! It really affected the way I saw myself, the way I saw others, and the way I learned. I eventually got over it, but I still cringe thinking about it. That's why I completely understand the importance of instilling proper self-esteem in children.

When a young child hears negative words about themselves, it manifests in who they become as an adult. Sometimes, an adult with no clear vision of their PURPOSE. Harmful words stay attached to children's hearts for years. Even when said in jest, telling a child *"You're stupid"* *"You're worthless - just like your daddy"* or *"How could you be so dumb?"* will senselessly chip away at their positive view of themselves. Sometimes, the damage is seemingly irreversible.

Oh, and when the negativity comes from good old Mom and Dad, it makes matters even worse! Children don't always know how to distinguish whether a statement is a joke or if it's truly what the parent believes about them. The world, the children at school, teachers or multiple influences outside of our homes give our kids enough challenges to deal with on a daily basis, so they need to have at least one place they can go to build healthy self-confidence.

Have you ever wondered why gang members consider each other family? Well, the culture of gangs is built on recruiting rejected children with negative home lives. When someone seems to build the self-confidence of a troubled kid whose spirit's been beaten down with negative words, the child is drawn in, with little to no regard for morality or danger. The child (hungry for positive attention) only sees that they are being "praised" for something, whether good or bad.

What happens in the house does not always stay there. So I submit to you - Mom and Dad that having a safe haven built upon positive reinforcement at home is crucial. Now I'm not suggesting that we praise our children for poor performance, but even when they fail at a task, give them hope that they have the potential to do *better*. (Kind of like our desire to grow and do better as parents, yes?). Building our children's self-image up at home lessens the impact of derogatory outside influences on their life. Show your child that you can love and nurture them better than the streets ever will! A few kind words can make a child feel as strong as David facing Goliath…and will put success in their eyes rather than defeat!

PURPOSE POINTS

Are you teaching your children that true peace is a quality you carry within yourself regardless of external circumstances?

_____

Have you taught your children that the path their life will take will be determined by the friends they keep and the friends they must say good-bye to?

_____

Have you taught your children that not every friendship you have in life will last? As our needs and wants change in life, so do our friendships.

PURPOSEFUL Listening

My wife, Isha often says, *"Distracted listening, is not listening at all."* And she's right. If you're raising children, chances are you often find yourself asking them, *"Are you listening?"*

Like receiving a compliment, rewards make kids feel good about themselves and their performance. So in our ministry, it's our PURPOSE to reward those children who come prepared and actually *listen* to the lessons being taught.

Listening (the main ingredient of *effective communication*) is the ability to accurately receive and interpret messages during the communication process. Not listening leads to mistakes, failure, wasted time and frustration for all parties involved. We've all been there. You know when the intent of the original message is misunderstood, leading to a complete breakdown in communication. Now everyone leaves the conversation *unhappy*. All because someone didn't take the time to listen.

Kids should be taught to differentiate between *listening* and *hearing*, which are actually two different worlds. Hearing refers to the *sound* of what's being said; listening requires *focus*. It means being aware of both verbal and non-verbal messages - not just paying attention to the story itself, but how the story is being told, the inflections in voice, and most importantly, body language.

Check out these tips to help teach kids proper listening etiquette:

1. Look at the person who is talking.
2. Sit or stand quietly.
3. Don't interrupt. Wait until the person is finished talking or seems like the child is disinterested or being rude.
4. Let the speaker know they're understood or ask questions if they are not.
5. Negative facial expressions during conversations are a no-no. Without a sour face, nod and occasionally chime in when appropriate.

Watch this: people who learn to *listen* tend to perform better on jobs and in school. Being good listeners reflects great home training and increases the probability that people will listen when we speak. Listening <u>well</u> helps us respond with the correct actions because now we have an understanding of expectations. *If you are having trouble listening, think of how you would feel if other people didn't listen to you.*

One more thing that may help - we should also teach the kiddos that when someone is giving them information they need for later (but may not remember), write it down. Effective listening is a skill that's underappreciated, but deserves more focus in the home.

PURPOSE in Honesty

"One isn't necessarily born with courage, but one is born with potential. Without courage we cannot practice any other virtue with consistency. We can't be kind, true, merciful, generous or honest" – *Maya Angelou*

In children's ministry, I can spot mayhem from miles away! And Friends, as long as we are parents I can guarantee you that at some point and time, our cute little angels may at least occasionally get into mischief. It's okay, though.

The advantage we have here as parents with PURPOSE is the prime opportunity to instill into our children that honesty is best when they've done something - whether it's good or bad. We can teach them to be honest and tell the truth about it, because honesty shows they can be trusted. If parents drop the sledgehammer approach and cultivate an environment in which children realize there will be consequences for their actions but Mom and Dad still love them, they're more likely to be honest about mischief. If people can *believe* what kids say, they're considered *trustworthy*.

Sometimes, adults will question children about their involvement in a situation. This is a terrific door opening for kids to give and have grace extended to them if we teach them the following easy principles of honesty:

1. *Look at the person.*
2. *Say exactly what happened if they're asked to provide information.*
3. *Answer any other questions. These can involve what they did or did not do, or what someone else did or did not do.*
4. *Don't leave out important facts.*
5. *Admit to mistakes or errors if they made them.*

Honesty leads to second chances. Now I realize we all make mistakes, but dishonesty leads to more problems – including earning the reputation of a liar, which is a great reason to tell the truth. Hey, being honest makes people *confident* that they've done the right thing!

It's difficult, and can seem like it's the easiest way out of a situation, but lying is not the answer; some people equate it to stealing or cheating. Besides, when people discover the lie, the consequences are far worse. Start by showing your kiddos how to use those effective communication skills we outlined earlier and they will resolve a lie with the truth sooner than later.

PURPOSE POINTS

If you could prevent your child from inheriting one bad behavioral habit from your spouse and one from yourself, which would it be?

_____

Do you know that you have the faith to do all God has planned for you to do as a parent?

_____

Are you teaching your children that Love at its highest level demands nothing in return?

PURPOSE in Constructive Discipline

Okay, now this is one of those topics that heats up conversations and sparks a multitude of varying opinions because most people are traditionally set in their ways on how it should be done: **DISCIPLINE.**

I once read a survey that stated, "More than half the parents believe that they use discipline effectively, but also believe that most parents are not strict enough." Interesting. Especially considering that the Bible itself tells us: "If you love your children you will correct them, if you don't love them you won't correct them." (Proverbs 13:24). Parents are to discipline their children just as God disciplines us.

Hey, I'm all about correction to maintain order in the house. But our PURPOSE as parents should never be punishment untempered with sound instruction. See while the disciplinary process can be painful, the results can be incredible – if we don't dish it out just because we can.

Check this little gem out in Hebrews 12: "If we learn to obey by being corrected, we will do right and live at peace." That's a wonderful promise for us as well as for our children. I remember during a leader's conference, a well-known preacher was asked, "If you could go back and do a particular thing over in your life, what would it be?" The preacher responded,

"As a parent I would try to see things through my children's eyes."

Wow.

Often, parents focus our attention almost entirely on our own concerns and agendas and fail to give our children the respect they deserve. We may even dive in with a harsh punishment to ease our frustrations with our kid's bad behavior, without considering the pressures they face that resulted in their acting out in the first place.

Our job as parents is not to force our children into an uncomfortable mold we've created for them, then discipline the child when they don't fit into it. Before we bring down the hammer, ask yourself - Did I take the time to sit down and discuss my child's actions with them? Did I allow him/her to *own* and stand by their opinions? Do they understand their actions, and does the situation really require punishment at all? Folks, we can't lead our children in the right direction without discovering who they are and respecting who God has created them to be.

And don't forget, God does not chastise without reason and warning. Discipline without these things is simply... bullying.

PURPOSE POINTS

It's not the Bible lying on your coffee table that makes the enemy flee, but the Word of God hidden in your heart, activated by the power of the Holy Spirit, and spoken in the appropriate situation.

A mirror reflects a man's face, but what he is really like is shown by the kind of friends he chooses.

When you as a parent has had a stressful day... exercise your "self-control" and don't take your frustrations out on your family.

If you had to identify the single biggest thing you fear for the future of your child what would you say?

If you could teach your child to do one thing at an unusually young age, what would it be?

If something were to happen to you and your spouse, who would you want to raise your children?

_____

If you were getting ready to explain the birds and the bees to your kids, how would you approach the task?

_____

If there were one adult you prefer to keep distant from your children, who would that be?

_____

If you were to identify the biggest obstacle to communication in your family right now, what would it be?

_____

A PURPOSEFUL Reality Check

A basic principle of good discipline requires that parents, teachers and other caretakers with PURPOSE have realistic expectations of what children are capable of doing.

Every Sunday, our ministry team asks the kiddos questions based on the lessons we're teaching them. Now of course we don't randomly quiz them out of the blue, because they haven't learned what's *expected* of them yet. Instead, we equip the kids with details on the topic first, then review it with them later.

Inappropriate expectations are a frequent problem in the parental community. It's obviously going to be crippling to the self-esteem of a child if they're not ready to do all the things we parents expect them to do. I mean, you don't try to toilet train a 12-month-old, expect a four- year-old to know multiplication tables, hope that your seven-year-old son and his four-year-old sister will stop fighting for good, or punish your three-year-old daughter because she can't clean up her room.

Let's take a little ***true or false*** quiz to see how your expectations are lining up.

Kids are naturally cooperative and unselfish. False! The younger child, the more selfish they are. They are out for themselves, and don't like it when you cross them, either. Kids are fun, affectionate and delightful when they get what they want. But when they don't? Whoo! Crying, screaming, whining and tantrums. And the child might do some of these things, too! (*Smile*). Get control of it, but don't hold it against them - that's just the way little kids are.

Kids are inherently rational. False! From birth, kids are more emotional and less rational. They are not little adults. Their ability to reason develops slowly and most often aggressively. on.

I should only have to tell them once. You're kidding, right? Discipline means training, and training means repetition. What children are learning has an intellectual aspect to it, but it also involves learning to emotionally tolerate frustration. Kids get the message (*communication, attitude, honesty, acceptance and No*) once they've rehearsed the actions over and over. Trust – repetition makes all the difference.

PURPOSE POINTS

If you had to explain the concept of ethics to your kids, how would you approach it?

———————————

If you could have prevented your child from being friends with one person while growing up, who would it have been?

———————————

If you had to pick the best television role model for your kids, who would it be? Why?

PURPOSE in Boundaries

It may be demanding, but part of parenting with PURPOSE implies that parents not only require more of their kids, but that they also expect more of themselves.

Friend, I hope you understand that parents can be emotionally available without discounting our role as authority figures in the lives of our children. Parents have a debilitating habit of believing that self-esteem and creativity are higher when children can *do their own thing* and not subjected to reasonable limits imposed upon them by adults.

No way!

Do you know kids perform and feel better about themselves (*creatively and otherwise*), when they learn the boundaries of reasonable behavior? The world has all kinds of limits and rules, that parents are responsible to introduce their kids to. Our kids may not like all the regulations we put in place, but somebody has to do it! If children don't recognize and work within these constraints, they will most likely get hurt badly in the long run.

Keep in mind, our kids are less likely to trust adults if they are consistently met with punishment rather than positive reinforcement. It's not all unpleasant or difficult, though. Kids love fun, so reward them with a cool activity when they successfully operate by the rules. One-on-one time (one child with one parent all to themselves) builds healthier family relationships and gives great balance to the discipline doled out when boundary lines are crossed.

Draw the line without ruling with an iron fist – trust, respect and appreciation will follow.

PURPOSE POINTS

If you could make one promise to your children that you are sure you will always keep what would it be?

———————————————

If you could ensure your child learned one moral lesson, what would it be?

———————————————

If you were to teach your child the principle of tolerance with an example, how would you do it?

PURPOSE in Aggravation

Parents, let's be realistic about our job!

You may think setting boundaries is tough, but in addition to having fun, feeding and being affectionate with our children, it's a little known fact that part of our PURPOSE is to aggravate our kids on a regular basis. No, really. It's part of the job!

Children are all super different, so some kids tolerate aggravation better than others. And few will ever say "*Thank you*" or show appreciation for their parent's hard work and effort. Many kids try to test and manipulate to get what they want. That's just a normal part of being a kid, and having to manage these times is just a normal part of being a parent.

As parents, our job is to lay a solid foundation in the lives of our children. This includes making sure our children are emotionally well-balanced, intellectually astute, physically healthy, spiritually attuned to the Gospel and enjoying a personal relationship with the Lord. It also means raising our children to have a firm and deep-rooted character that is nurtured by the principles found in God's Word.

REMEMBER: give them all the love and care they need, but you must regularly aggravate your kids because that's part of the job.

...they may even thank you for it later!

PURPOSE POINTS

If you could successfully instill three values above all others in your children, which would you want them to be?

_____

If you had to explain the meanings of love and hate to your child, how would you do it?

_____

If you were to decide to make your child do one thing or have one experience against their wishes, for their own good, what would it be?

PURPOSE in Clarity

*"**Behave yourself**!" "**Leave your brother alone**!"*
*"**I thought I told you to clean your room**!"*

N*ow,* aggravating our children may be scribbled across our daily To Do lists, *but if you've* caught yourself saying these things to him/her "a thousand times" …you may need to review your expectations of your child and, more importantly - how you communicate them with PURPOSE.

Don't be shocked when we don't get the results we think they're going to get. The biggest excuse kids have for not doing what we want them to is t*hey didn't understa*nd. That means either we need to revisit the effective listening skills we implemented a few chapters back, or we just aren't clear enough about our expectations. At any rate, this would be a great time to sit down with your child and define behavioral expectations both in and out of your home.

In *othe*r words: **say** what you mean, and mea*n what you say*.

Parental RULE #1: Be CLEAR. Instead of saying, "Please clean up your room," be more specific: "*Please make up your bed and pick your clothes up off of the floor.*" Or, "*Be home by 6:00*" rather than "*Don't be late.*" Lack of clarity leaves the door wide open for misunderstandings (accidental and otherwise) so be intentional with the words you used to give a directive to your child.

*The second parental rule (especially important w*ith strong-willed children), is to tell your child what will happen if they don't *comply with your command: "If you don't wear your helmet, y*ou're not riding your bike." Or to keep things positive, you *can try something like, "If you want to ride your bike, I expect you to us*e your helmet at all times."

This practice generally hits the ball out of the park for me. You get the picture, and the kiddos will certainly get the point!

PURPOSE POINTS

If there were one still-living public figure
who you'd propose as a role model for your
children, who would take the honor?

_____

If you were to name the one ingredient that is most
critical for your child's education, what would you say?

_____

If you could prevent your children from getting
into one of life's ruts, which would you want them
to avoid, and how would you help them do it?

PURPOSE in Rules

Each of the suggestions I have provided thus far have a single common denominator to help serve their PURPOSE: each requires RULES to execute.

Well balanced kids cannot function without some type of regulations. Can you imagine coming to pick your child up from daycare or children's church in the middle of chaotic free-will? Neither can I.

Focus on the behavior. Don't shame or embarrass your *child into behaving by saying, "When are you going* to grow up?" Instead, tell them: "I want you to stop taking *apart your* sister's dolls." Be specific an*d direct. For example, instead of saying, "It's bedtim*e," your directive should be: "It's 9:00 p.m.; please go upstairs to take your shower."

Use your normal voice instead of raising it; screaming shows your child that you're not in *control. Don't sound irri*tated; speak with a firm, matter-of-fact voice that says, "You're going to do XYZ now."

Explain what will happen if the rules are broken, and allow your child to make an informed choice whenever possible. Most importantly, if he/she does break the rules, parents must follow through with the stated consequence.

The bottom line is that children need us to be clear about our rules and expectations, and they need to know that their actions - good and bad, will have consequences. If kids choose to break the rules, then they choose to deal with the consequences. Even more so, if parents choose the right words when we talk to our kids, we may find that getting them to follow the rules is much less stressful for everyone!

Sometimes children don't do what we ask of them because we're not clear enough with our message. Think about how you can change your language to gain better cooperation from your child in a situation that you often deal with to keep it from escalating.

PURPOSE POINTS

If you were to state the most valuable thing you hope to leave your children, what would it be?

_____

If you were to take your kids somewhere to teach them a moral lesson, where would you go, and for what lesson?

_____

If there were one person your kids should always listen to, other than their parents, who would it be?

PURPOSE in Monitoring

Do you make it your PURPOSE to know what your child listens to and reads? What about how he/she spends time with their friends?

I enjoy knowing what's going on with my son and the world around him. His acceptance of my consistent involvement reflects in his positive behavior and leadership skills. Talking with your child about their interests opens up a world of opportunity for you to share your values, which they will most likely emulate.

Monitoring their activities lowers the chances of children getting involved in situations their parents don't approve of - especially harmful ones.

Unsupervised children simply have more opportunities to experiment with risky behaviors, including the use of alcohol, tobacco, and illegal drugs, potentially starting substance abuse at earlier ages. Not to mention, luxury technology such as Web sites, blogs, Xbox, PS3, tablets and cell phones can also threaten to expose children to dangerous drugs and put them in contact with dealers or sexual predators.

Mom and Dad, need to monitor our children's activities and help them navigate away from temptations in the digital world. It's our responsibility as parents to ensure our children are covered and protected from some of the social ills and predators that threaten to derail them from living in God's purpose.

Communication, honesty, boundaries, rules and involvement – they all work together for the good of our children!

PURPOSE POINTS

If you could teach your children how to deal
with mistakes, or provide them with a philosophy
for mistakes, how would you do it?

_____

If you were to finish the phrase "My children
respect me because," how would it read?

_____

If you were to recommend a way to teach kids they can do
anything they put their mind to, what would you say?

PURPOSE in Television

Okay, I'm just going to say it like this: We can't go building up all this communication and boundaries, regulations so on and so forth, then leave little Timmy locked up in his bedroom watching who knows what on the television! It defeats our PURPOSE.

By high school graduation, most children will have spent more hours watching TV than learning in the classroom. Kids are influenced by the thousands of commercials they see each year, many of which advertise alcohol, junk food, fast foods, and toys. And guess what? Part of monitoring what our kids are up to includes checking out what they're watching on the tube.

Children think it's great to have their own television in their bedroom, because *"all [their] friends have one."* Nature programs, historical documentaries, game shows that test your mind - it's all good stuff on *your* television, but you need to check out what's on your kid's TV. Have you seen the kind of stuff on there lately? Frankly, it's harder for adults to monitor what the kids are watching if they are hiding out in the bedroom. But take heart! You can control the use of TV in your home so it's a source of entertainment and education for your family and not an electronic babysitter that includes violent situations and foul language.

Many programs have adult content, so it's not healthy for young children to spend too much time watching the TV alone. Your guidance and support is important to your children's healthy development. Real talk Mom, Dad - if your kids are not being taught by you, their behavior/attitude might be developed from something they've seen on the screen.

Be a good example. Spend your own free time on activities other than watching TV, like reading, working on a hobby, or gardening.

Society's massive addiction to social media, television, gaming and other distractions may be hard to draw away from, but it can be done. The level of discipline every parent must implement in *raising purpose driven children may seem extremist* to some folk, but that's not the case. You are just being intentional and sensitive to anything that can hinder your child from living their best life.

In the words of the late Dr. Myles Munroe's mother, "If you watch too much TV, you'll never be on TV."

PURPOSE POINTS

If you were to name the one thing you'd most like your kids to say "No" to, what would you pick?

_____

If there were one question you'd like to ask your child but haven't, what would it be?

_____

If you had to name one suspicion that would cause you to read your child's mail or search their room, what do you think it would be?

PURPOSEFUL Activities

Sports. Dance. Theater. Art. There are endless creative outlets for kids to express themselves and identify their own PURPOSE; a slew of them are even offered after school!

Participating in organized afterschool activities helps children cement many of the values we've discussed instilling in them throughout this manual. They meet new friends (communication), as well as lean new skills (discipline, rules, and boundaries). Now, some after school activities may wreak a little havoc on the pocketbook, but there are so many others that are offered free.

Public schools should able to help you locate affordable and appropriate activities for your children. Decide what activities are feasible, and ask your child to choose one or more. Some shy children may hesitate, but explain that just like school, afterschool activities are an important part of growing up and reiterate their options.

Here's where those boundaries we talked about come in to play. Once your child chooses an activity, clearly communicate your expectation that they will stick it out for the year and at the beginning of the next school year, they can make a different choice if they want to. I would say, though, that if you have good evidence that the activity is poorly supervised or that the adult supervisors are abusive to the children…do not pass go and get your child out of there! You can avoid such problems by carefully screening the activities before you give your children a choice to join in or by volunteering to supervise the activity if time permits. During the year when children express reluctance to continue with the activity, quietly remind them that they will have another choice next year.

PURPOSE POINTS

What after school activities are your children involved in?

_____

How can you help them get involved if they are not?

_____

What should you do when a child wants to discontinue an activity before the school year is over.

PURPOSE in Providing

"...After all, children should not have to save up
for their parents, but parents for their children."
~2 Corinthians 12:14

My son does not write the check for our family's mortgage. That's not his PURPOSE. He's not old enough to have a driver's license, so there's no need for him to worry with taking care of our car note. See, God intended for parents to provide the material needs of their family. It's inappropriate for children to take on the burden of how the family is going to make it until the end of the month or where their next meal is going to come from. Being a parent means committing to our children's material welfare. This means we have to make decisions based on our child's needs rather than our own.

Isha and I can both look back on time when we spent money that was not *spare cash* to help our son with something that would be of lasting value to him. Raising our family on modest incomes forced us to create very tight, no-frills budgets. When one month's money was gone, we waited until the following moth for additional funds.

Of course, providing for children requires balance. We don't want to burden our kids with the details of the family's day-to-day survival, but we also don't want to make things too easy for them. Coddling can make them self-centered and selfish.

Realistically, we should assign our children some chores around the house to give them an opportunity to earn a weekly allowance, rather than just handing them money whenever they ask, regardless of their behavior. If kids work for their cash, they'll learn to manage their funds wisely. Parents – YOU take care of the bills and relieve your kids of unnecessary stress; let them concentrate on being a kid. Parents expect children to remain in a child's place...but we can't expect them to do so when we place them in adult positions. I'd much rather my son enjoys a happy childhood, than force him into early adulthood.

PURPOSE in One-on-One Time

One day it could happen to YOU. That dreaded time when…your child now feels they are too old to be hanging out with Mom and Dad – and still remain cool. But don't fret…you still serve PURPOSE in their life.

So as our kids get older, how can we "old" folk (i.e., The *Parentals*) stay in touch with them as they mature and it seems like now they want to spend more time with friends than us? Or when they *are* home, they're in their bedroom, phone attached to their hands or computer commanding all of their attention.

One-on-one fun without the entire family is a good start. Your older child may not want to eat dinner with the family, and family outings may not be on their agenda. But dinner and a movie, a shopping excursion, or driving around in the car - just the two of you - may help a lot. Let your spouse stay home with the other kids. This is a principle my family practices in our own home. Isha and I enjoy taking turns getting to know the person our child is becoming, and he appreciates spending time with us.

My Friends, time is a hot commodity that unfortunately, we never seem to have enough of. Take the time to *spend* time with your children.

A PURPOSEFUL Vision

Write the vision, make it plain and watch your PURPOSE manifest.

Do you dream with your child?

One of the best things we as parents can do to help shape our kid's future is to dream with them. Those young, impressionable years are the absolute best time to share with them the hope and vision for what you hope their life will be like in the future, and allow them to share their own vision with you. Include your love and loving relationship as part of it.

Sharing the vision doesn't mean that you should sit and dictate your child's career choices or what they *need to do* with their life. Gently insist that your child prepare for his future by acquiring certain skills, from learning to making his own bed to staying in school. But mostly, take delight in your child as they discover their own potential and make decisions about their own paths.

Pop quiz: remember what I mentioned previously about building your child's self-esteem? Well, this is one of those times you can strap on your construction gear and start building! Imagine the future out loud with your child:

"I can't wait to see what our lives will be like fifty years from now."

"What kind of car do you think you'll be driving?"

"I look forward to the day when you will invite me to your house for dinner."

"I hope we laugh and have a good time in your kitchen, just like we do now. I wonder what you'll cook. What do you think? Hot dogs or hamburgers"?

"I'm going to miss you when you go off to college. There will be nothing for me to find stuffed under your bed. And it's going to be much quieter. I'm not even going to know how to act being able to use the phone whenever I want! It's going to be fun though, to see what major you choose."

Create a vision board together, detailing your protections of a future loving relationship into the casual course of everyday life. Let your children begin to imagine the close parent-child relationship you will have in future and let him/her know that you expect to be a part of their life. Don't get me wrong, Mom and Dad - I'm not saying draw yourself a bedroom in your kid's future six-bedroom home, but do let them know you'll still be there for them, no matter how much time goes by.

PURPOSE POINTS

Are you focused on helping your children become adults who can face the world in competent and remarkable ways?

———————————————

Are you being a living example that you want your children to meet and exceed in their future life?

———————————————

Always be careful to check the area to make sure that it is "childproof."

———————————————

PURPOSE in Consequences

You're on the phone, so your child knows you're distracted. It's almost dinnertime, but he goes to grab a few cookies, and you catch him. He knows the rule is no cookies before dinner. Do you tell your friend "excuse me" and in a sweet voice say, "Johnny, I said no cookies before dinner" and let him get away with it, or do you firmly say "Johnny, put those cookies back or you can forget about ice cream tonight" (his evening ritual)?

Although this may seem like a pretty harmless situation, you and your child each have two choices. If you let him get away with it, he learns there are times when he can break the rules. On the other hand, if you tell him that he has two choices, he learns (1) that you mean business and (2) that his choices have consequences.

You guys know by now (just from reading this book) that I believe in lists to plainly see your PURPOSE in front of your own eyes. Here's a few helpful hints about executing consequences to help you stand firm when your kids cross the boundary lines you've drawn out for them.

Follow through. Follow through with the consequences you've established for rulebreaking no matter what. If your child breaks the rules, then they should have a clear understanding of what's next to come, right? Failing to follow through sends the message that your rules aren't important and it's okay to break them.

Be consistent. *"C'mon, just this one time?"* Have you ever let the ball drop with this plea? Remember that consistency reinforces for your child the type of behavior expected of them. Similarly, if you discipline your child one day for talking back but ignore the same behavior the next, they learn that sometimes they can get away with being disrespectful.

If you don't mean it, don't say it. Sometimes children can get us so angry that, in the heat of the moment, we state a consequence that we know we're not going to follow through with, at least not entirely. Make sure you're willing to do what you say. If you won't really ground your child for a month, then don't say you will. It weakens your effectiveness when you ease up later.

Remember: Part of honesty…includes reliability in what we mean and say.

PURPOSE POINTS

During school holidays, how will you
manage with work and your child?

_____

Teach your child that they might think you're smart
when you get out of college, but I suggest that
the real education is only just the beginning.

_____

Can your child predict with 100% accuracy what
will happen as a result of their misbehavior?

PURPOSE in Control

Who exactly is in control, here?

Children can't be trained if they can't be controlled. Nothing bothers me more than seeing a two-year-old running the entire family. If the toddler doesn't want to go where the family planned, then everybody stays home. If the kid steals toys from a neighbor, the parents lie to cover up for their little terror. When the two-year-old is caught hitting other kids with a bat, the parents accuse the victims of provoking their sweet little baby. Everyone is controlled by this two-year-old menace!

Training your child will often have to be a forceful (but not regrettable) situation. God has ordained an instrument PURPOSED for you to use in order to administer control over your child. And he has provided a strategic and well-paddled area on your child's body to receive this instrument. Of course, the divine instrument of love is the rod. "He who spares his rod hates his son, but he who loves him disciplines him promptly." (Proverbs 13:24).

Basically, you gotta get the little joker! In all seriousness, though, if you want to obey God, you have no choice. Use the rod if you love your child. Can't bring yourself to use the rod? Then you might as well tell your kids that you hate them. That's what God says.

I want you to notice that He says in His Word "Chasten him betimes." This means often - as often as he needs it. Don't try to beat your child with words. Browbeating will never replace bottom beating, and only causes mental abuse. But because faith comes by hearing, negative words plant faith that he is a failure in his heart.

Many parents use alternate methods in disciplining their kids. In this era, you hear different psychiatrists spouting all kinds of disciplinary theories that many parents are willing to try. But God's word is much better than any psychology and God's word says a child should be spanked! Teach your children to regard the paddle as an instrument of love not punishment. In fact, use a positive vocabulary with your children. Don't talk about punishment but about training.

…and <u>never</u> use your hands to discipline your child.

Your hands should be used to communicate affection. God never uses his hands to hit us but to welcome us lovingly into his presence. What a surprise we would have if we were expecting him to hug us and he slapped us instead. If you discipline with your hands, your child won't know whether you're going to love on him or hit him.

Sparing the rod tells our kids Mom and Dad don't have time to train them up in the way they should go, but discipline shows them we care.

PURPOSE in Unconditional Love

The time to make the greatest impression on children is when they are young.

Though it is never *too late to become good parents, the* earlier we lay a strong foundation for our children the better off our children will be. Our groundwork transcends through childhood, adolescence, teen years, and adulthood. More than anyone else, as parents we are entrusted with both the opportunity and responsibility to positively influence our children's lives. More than anything, I believe that all parents owe it to their child to give them the one thing they need most: unconditional love.

The key to a good parent-child relationship is the willingness to love and accept your children solely because they are your PURPOSE. This should not be reliant upon behavior, talent, performance, potential or anything else.

Remember the story of the Prodigal Son? The father never gave up on his son didn't reject him for his poor decision making. He never said "I told you so" or "I hope you didn't get anyone pregnant" and didn't even compare his wayward son to his brother who remained home. He simply loved his son, kissed him and celebrated his return. When we offer this type of unconditional love to our children, it provides them with a nurturing environment where they grow emotionally, psychologically and physically secure.

Consistent displays of unconditional love can help in the development of the intimate parent-child relationship we talked about envisioning in the future, where children are comfortable sharing hopes and dreams and fears and failures. And actively displaying this steadfast love toward our children pays dividends during even their most difficult years.

PURPOSE in Structure

Family Planning Program

Commit to the Lord whatever you do, and your
plans will succeed. Proverbs 16:3

In your pursuit to develop good habits, the following questions
should be answered to yield plans for success:

1. What do we want to accomplish as a family?

    _____

2. Who do we need to help us accomplish this?

    _____

3. Where can we go for more information?

    _____

4. What books, magazines or journals do we need to read?

    _____

5. Who should we associate with?

    _____

6. How long should it take?

   _____

7. How much will it cost?

   _____

8. What courses should we take?

   _____

9. Where can we get experience?

   _____

10. What do we have now?

   _____

Striving for PURPOSE

Goal-Setting Program

God will direct your steps when you make a
concrete plan to move toward what you desire.

My age: _____ Today's Date: _____

Name: _____

By God's grace, I commit to accomplishing the following
goals this year:

Personal Spiritual Goals

1. _____
2. _____
3. _____
4. _____

Personal Family Goals

1. _____
2. _____
3. _____
4. _____

Personal Health Goals

1. _____
2. _____
3. _____
4. _____

Personal Academic Goals

1. _____
2. _____
3. _____
4. _____

Personal Career Goals

1. _____
2. _____
3. _____
4. _____

Personal Relationship Goals

1. _____
2. _____
3. _____
4. _____

Personal Financial Goals

1. _____
2. _____
3. _____
4. _____

Personal Investment Goals

1. _____
2. _____
3. _____

Guidance with PURPOSE

SCRIPTURES TO REMEMBER

(ALL VERSES TAKEN FROM King James Version)

Ephesians 6:1-3

"Children, obey your parents in the Lord, for this is right. ² "Honor your father and mother"—which is the first commandment with a promise— ³ "so that it may go well with you and that you may enjoy long life on the earth."

Ephesians 6:4

Fathers, [b] do not exasperate your children; instead, bring them up in the training and instruction of the Lord.

Deuteronomy 11:19

Teach them to your children, talking about them when you sit at home and when you walk along the road, when you lie down and when you get up

Deuteronomy 21:18-21

If a man has a stubborn and rebellious son, which will not obey the voice of his father, or the voice of his mother, and that, when they have chastened him, will not hearken unto them:

[19] Then shall his father and his mother lay hold on him, and bring him out unto the elders of his city, and unto the gate of his place;

[20] And they shall say unto the elders of his city, This our son is stubborn and rebellious, he will not obey our voice; he is a glutton, and a drunkard.

[21] And all the men of his city shall stone him with stones, that he die: so shalt thou put evil away from among you; and all Israel shall hear, and fear

Deuteronomy 6:7

Impress them on your children. Talk about them when you sit at home and when you walk along the road, when you lie down and when you get up.

Deuteronomy 4:9-10

Only be careful, and watch yourselves closely so that you do not forget the things your eyes have seen or let them fade from your heart as long as you live. Teach them to your children and to their children after them. [10] Remember the day you stood before the LORD your God at Horeb, when he said to me, "Assemble the people before me to hear my words so that they may learn to revere me as long as they live in the land and may teach them to their children."

Deuteronomy 11:19

Teach them to your children, talking about them when you sit at home and when you walk along the road, when you lie down and when you get up.

Isaiah 38:19

The living, the living--they praise you, as I am doing today; parents tell their children about your faithfulness.

Isaiah 54:13

And all thy children shall be taught of the LORD; and great shall be the peace of thy children.

1ˢᵗ Timothy 5:8

Anyone who does not provide for their relatives, and especially for their own household, has denied the faith and is worse than an unbeliever.

1ˢᵗ Timothy 3:4

He must manage his own family well and see that his children obey him, and he must do so in a manner worthy of full respect.

Hebrews 12:7

Endure hardship as discipline; God is treating you as his children. For what children are not disciplined by their father? [8] If you are not disciplined—and everyone undergoes discipline—then you are not legitimate, not true sons and daughters at all.

Hebrews 11:20

By faith Isaac blessed Jacob and Esau in regard to their future.

Genesis 24:1-4

Abraham was now very old, and the LORD had blessed him in every way. [2] He said to the senior servant in his household, the one in charge of all that he had, "Put your hand under my thigh. [3] I want you to swear by the LORD, the God of heaven and the God of earth, that you will not get a wife for my son from the daughters of the Canaanites, among whom I am living, [4] but will go to my country and my own relatives and get a wife for my son Isaac."

Genesis 28:1-2

Then Isaac called Jacob and blessed him and directed him, "You must not take a wife from the Canaanite women. [2] Arise, go to Paddan-aram to the house of Bethuel your mother's father, and take as your wife from there one of the daughters of Laban your mother's brother.

Genesis 17:18

[8] And Abraham said to God, "If only Ishmael might live under your blessing!

Genesis 48:15

Then he blessed Joseph and said,

"May the God before whom my fathers Abraham and Isaac walked faithfully, the God who has been my shepherd all my life to this day,

Genesis 18:19

[19] For I have chosen him, so that he will direct his children and his household after him to keep the way of the LORD by doing what is right and just, so that the LORD will bring about for Abraham what he has promised him."

1 Chronicles 29:19

And give my son Solomon the wholehearted devotion to keep your commands, statutes and decrees and to do everything to build the palatial structure for which I have provided.

1 Chronicles 28:9

[9] "And you, my son Solomon, acknowledge the God of your father, and serve him with wholehearted devotion and with a willing mind, for the Lord searches every heart and understands every desire and every thought. If you seek him, he will be found by you; but if you forsake him, he will reject you forever.

Job 1:5

And it was so, when the days of their feasting were gone about, that Job sent and sanctified them, and rose up early in the morning, and offered burnt offerings according to the number of them all: for Job said, It may be that my sons have sinned, and cursed God in their hearts. Thus did Job continually.

Job 42:15

Nowhere in all the land were there found women as beautiful as Job's daughters, and their father granted them an inheritance along with their brothers.

2 Samuel 12:16

David pleaded with God for the child. He fasted and spent the nights lying in sackcloth on the ground.

Mark 5:23

He pleaded earnestly with him, "My little daughter is dying. Please come and put your hands on her so that she will be healed and live."

Matthew 18:12-14

What do you think? If a man owns a hundred sheep, and one of them wanders away, will he not leave the ninety-nine on the hills and go to look for the one that wandered off? [13] And if he finds it, truly I tell you, he is happier about that one sheep than about the ninety-nine that did not wander off. [14] In the same way your Father in heaven is not willing that any of these little ones should perish.

Mathew 18:26

He called a little child and had him stand among them.

And he said: "I tell you the truth, unless you change and become like little children, you will never enter the kingdom of heaven.

Therefore, whoever humbles himself like this child is the greatest in the kingdom of heaven.

"And whoever welcomes a little child like this in my name welcomes me.

But if anyone causes one of these little ones who believe in me to sin, it would be better for him to have a large millstone hung around his neck and to be drowned in the depths of the sea.

Matthew 19:13-14

[13] Then people brought little children to Jesus for him to place his hands on them and pray for them. But the disciples rebuked them.

[14] Jesus said, "Let the little children come to me, and do not hinder them, for the kingdom of heaven belongs to such as these."

John 9:3-5

"Neither this man nor his parents sinned," said Jesus, "but this happened so that the works of God might be displayed in him. [4] As long as it is day, we must do the works of him who sent me. Night is coming, when no one can work. [5] While I am in the world, I am the light of the world."

Luke 2:48-52

When his parents saw him, they were astonished. His mother said to him, "Son, why have you treated us like this? Your father and I have been anxiously searching for you."

[49] "Why were you searching for me?" he asked. "Didn't you know I had to be in my Father's house?"[a] [50] But they did not understand what he was saying to them.

[51] Then he went down to Nazareth with them and was obedient to them. But his mother treasured all these things in her heart. [52] And Jesus grew in wisdom and stature, and in favor with God and man.

Luke 18:29

"Truly I tell you," Jesus said to them, "no one who has left home or wife or brothers or sisters or parents or children for the sake of the kingdom of God

2 Corinthians 12:14-15

[14] Now I am ready to visit you for the third time, and I will not be a burden to you, because what I want is not your possessions but you. After all, children should not have to save up for their parents, but parents for their children. [15] So I will very gladly spend for you everything I have and expend myself as well. If I love you more, will you love me less?

Colossians 3:20-21

Children, obey your parents in everything, for this pleases the Lord. Fathers,[a] do not embitter your children, or they will become discouraged.

Leviticus 19:3

'each of you must respect your mother and father, and you must observe my Sabbaths. I am the LORD your God.

Exodus 20:12

[12] "Honor your father and your mother, so that you may live long in the land the LORD your God is giving you.

Exodus 21:15-17

[5] And he that smiteth his father, or his mother, shall be surely put to death.

[16] And he that stealeth a man, and selleth him, or if he be found in his hand, he shall surely be put to death.

[17] And he that curseth his father, or his mother, shall surely be put to death.

Exodus 10:2

That you may tell your children and grandchildren how I dealt harshly with the Egyptians and how I performed my signs among them, and that you may know that I am the LORD."

Titus 2:3-5

Likewise, teach the older women to be reverent in the way they live, not to be slanderers or addicted to much wine, but to teach what is good. [4] Then they can urge the younger women to love their husbands and children, [5] to be self-controlled and pure, to be busy at home, to be kind, and to be subject to their husbands, so that no one will malign the word of God.

Joel 1:2-3

Hear this, you elders; listen, all who live in the land. Has anything like this ever happened in your days or in the days of your ancestors?

[3] Tell it to your children, and let your children tell it to their children, and their children to the next generation.

Proverbs 10:1

A wise son brings joy to his father, but a foolish son brings grief to his mother.

Proverbs 22:6

Start children off on the way they should go, and even when they are old they will not turn from it.

Proverbs 13:24

whoever spares the rod hates their children, but the one who loves their children is careful to discipline them.

Proverbs 19:18

Discipline your children, for in that there is hope; do not be a willing party to their death.

Proverbs 29:17

Discipline your children, and they will give you peace; they will bring you the delights you desire.

Proverbs 1:8-9

Listen, my son, to your father's instruction and do not forsake your mother's teaching.

[9] They are a garland to grace your head and a chain to adorn your neck.

Proverbs 30:17

"The eye that mocks a father, that scorns an aged mother, will be pecked out by the ravens of the valley, will be eaten by the vultures.

Proverbs 7:1-3

My son, keep my words and store up my commands within you.

[2] Keep my commands and you will live guard my teachings as the apple of your eye.

[3] Bind them on your fingers; write them on the tablet of your heart.

Proverbs 22:15

Folly is bound up in the heart of a child, but the rod of discipline will drive it far away.

Proverbs 23:13-14

Do not withhold discipline from a child; if you punish them with the rod, they will not die.

[14] Punish them with the rod and save them from death.

Proverbs 29:15

A rod and a reprimand impart wisdom, but a child left undisciplined disgraces its mother.

Proverbs 29:17

Discipline your children, and they will give you peace; they will bring you the delights you desire.

Psalms 112:1-2

Praise the LORD.[b] Blessed are those who fear the LORD, who find great delight in his commands.

[2] Their children will be mighty in the land; the generation of the upright will be blessed.

Psalms 127:3-5

Children are a heritage from the LORD, offspring a reward from him.

⁴ Like arrows in the hands of a warrior are children born in one's youth.

⁵ Blessed is the man whose quiver is full of them. They will not be put to shame when they contend with their opponents in court.

Psalms 139:13-16

For you created my inmost being; you knit me together in my mother's womb.

¹⁴ I praise you because I am fearfully and wonderfully made; your works are wonderful, I know that full well.

¹⁵ My frame was not hidden from you when I was made in the secret place, when I was woven together in the depths of the earth.

¹⁶ Your eyes saw my unformed body; all the days ordained for me were written in your book before one of them came to be.

Psalm 103:13

As a father has compassion on his children, so the LORD has compassion on those who fear him;

Psalms 78:2-8

I will open my mouth in a parable; I will utter dark sayings of old,

³ Which we have heard and known, And our fathers have told us.

⁴ We will not hide *them* from their children, Telling to the generation to come the praises of the LORD, And His strength and His wonderful works that He has done.

[5] For He established a testimony in Jacob, And appointed a law in Israel, Which He commanded our fathers, That they should make them known to their children;

[6] That the generation to come might know *them,* The children *who* would be born, *That* they may arise and declare *them* to their children,

[7] That they may set their hope in God, And not forget the works of God, But keep His commandments;

[8] And may not be like their fathers, A stubborn and rebellious generation, A generation *that* did not set its heart aright, And whose spirit was not faithful to God.

A Man of PURPOSE

ABOUT THE AUTHOR

"Where Purpose is Unknown Abuse is Inevitable" — Dr. Myles Munroe

Fatherless, hopeless, lost, wounded, exposed to violence and gang activity which could have ultimately led to self-destruction — all snares to destroy a man ... but God! Pastor Ricardo Miller, Sr. has ministered for two decades and traveled the world inspiring everyone from government officials, educators, church leaders, to youth and children as well as many others from all walks of life.

"Before I formed you in the womb I knew you; before you were born I sanctified you; I ordained you a prophet to the nations." — Jeremiah 1:5

Pastor Miller is impacting thousands of youth globally. His wisdom, obedience and faith have led him to the destiny that God ordained for his life. Despite a few obstacles, he never accepted defeat because he fought for his purpose.

A native of Nassau, Bahamas, he embraced his calling at the age of 18. Before that however, his lifestyle as a gang leader nearly cost him everything. Not to mention, how his rebellious nature as a teen almost hindered him from graduating with his senior class. He graduated with only an attendance certificate. He later returned to school to obtain his diploma in addition to attending evening classes to develop his academic skills.

Pastor Miller was raised solely by his mother and never knew his father.

"My mother was a single parent with five kids," he shared. "Despite her being a single parent, I wanted to get married and have kids with my wife. You have to have a dream that's bigger than you and what you want. To achieve it, you have to do whatever it takes to make it happen."

Having a family was important to Pastor Miller, and he achieved his dream by marrying the love of his life, Isha. Together they have one son, Ricardo, Jr.

Rather than giving in to the statistics that society has placed on single-parent households, Pastor Miller was determined to beat the odds.

"I could have used my upbringing as a crutch or an excuse to justify why I couldn't make it. I decided that it doesn't matter how I start; it's how I finish." He continued, "It's not where I am; it's where I'm going. I made a conscious decision to not live life full of excuses. I used my situation as motivating factors to show the enemy he is a liar and that God has had a plan for my life since the beginning — and I'm going to finish well."

Pastor Miller knew he was a leader, but he had used that gift negatively. Internally, he recognized he wasn't helping others transform positively. After surrendering his life to Christ, his leadership skills began to evolve. He volunteered in the church as well as several community activities. He realized if he wanted to help the community, he had to start at the base by reaching the youth and children.

"The key is to start with children before they're at a stage where you have to break bad habits or start habits that need to be broken." He shared, "I wanted to start with children to help them avoid the pitfalls I was involved in and so many others."

Pastor Miller's mission is to help others discover their purpose. He empowers a generation to understand who they are and whose they are. His goal is to train others to maximize their purpose and live life effectively. He believes we're living in a time where many young people are unaware of personal identity.

"Where purpose is unknown abuse is inevitable," he says, "so I'm on a mission to help others discover purpose."

Pastor Miller is compelled to see a life change in people, especially youth and children. As a leader in ministry for over 20 years, he can reflect on the impact he has made on others. He has seen transformation in college graduates, high school students, preteens and children.

"To witness children I impacted return to share the message I ministered to help them, it drives and motivates me to break generational curses," he says. "As my grandmother and mother would say, 'I don't have to live in the standards I was brought up in. To see what God has done in my life, I know what He can do in others' lives as well."

One of his most difficult challenges was dropping out of high school and being unable to read. He accepted his deficiencies and knew they had to be addressed. Returning to school at 18 was challenging because he had to let go of his pride.

"For me to be the man God wanted me to be, I knew I had to let go of being in denial," he shared.

He hired a tutor and attended night courses. He worked extremely hard to make up the years he lost in high school. He realized that if God gave him life, He gave it to him for a reason.

"If you don't know your purpose, you're going to abuse the life you've been given," he said. Young people need to understand that there's purpose within each one of them. The failure to not understand the purpose is to abuse one's life. Regardless of your circumstances, you can fulfill your God-ordained purpose. Despite the situation, you're in, something good can come out of this. You have to surround yourself with people who will inspire you to want to change for the better," he avers.???

He believes everyone was created for a purpose.

"Your parents are in your life to help you, but beyond that it's up to you. God can still do amazing things in your life, but you have to want it," he said.

Pastor Miller has launched a campaign to reach young people around the world. The THINK NEXT GENERATION Tour is being hosted across the United States, Caribbean and Central America and Africa. Think Next Generation epitomizes "children you're next.". His organization, Ricardo Miller Children's Ministries, focuses on first through fifth graders and partners with churches to help them understand that if they're not reaching children, they're missing the future.

"We target three important factors: (1) Children, by helping capture their purpose. (2) Parents, in challenging them to understand how to help young people discover their purpose and train them in the way they should go. Most importantly, to understand that we train them in the way *they* were designed to go and not the way *we* want them to go. *"Train up a child in the way he should go, And when he is old he will not depart from it."* Proverbs 22:6.

He continued, "(3) Workers, such as teachers, ministers and Sunday school teachers on how to influence young people effectively. The key is to listen to them so they can maximize their potential. Many students aren't listening to the teachers and we're losing our young people. Any church not reaching the children is a dying church. It's only a matter of time before they become irrelevant. We have to do everything we can to impact the world and reach our children first and foremost. If the future is to be changed, children are the agency through whom change will come," he stated.

The Think Next Generation Tour, hosted by Ricardo Miller Children's Ministries includes workshop training sessions to equip workers to effectively reach youth and children. He said, "Statistics show we are losing our children and not reaching new children. Any entity which is losing children and not attracting new children will eventually become obsolete. If we're going to be a church of the future we have to focus on our youth and children and connect with them in an appropriate way."

WHAT LEADERS ARE SAYING ABOUT RICARDO MILLER

As the CEO of the largest "personality driven" Internet (Radio) Network in the world, I am always looking to learn about empowering life strategies. I have attended Ricardo Miller's sessions and I can say with 100% confidence that what and how he teaches, not only is inspiring and informational in nature, but most importantly, life changing when applied. Not only, is he a great leader in the movement for empowering churches through developing amazing children's ministries, he is also a great at communicator, leader, and motivator for anyone who wants to reach their highest potential.

Sylvia "Sammi" Martinez
Fishbowl Radio Network
Arlington, Texas

An answered prayer for Christian parents all over the world! Pastor Ricardo Miller has exceeded all expectations of what leading a 21st Century Children's Ministry should be. Now he is leading the entire family in the exact same direction with his new book "Parenting With A Purpose", an innovative and inspirational guide for the next generation. Pastor Ricardo provides relevant and timely principles to arm parents with the tools necessary to raise our children in a world where so many influences can distract and take our kids away from their God given purpose. "Parenting with a Purpose" shatters those distractions and gives parents and children what they need not only from God but the practical things needed to thrive in life.

Naomi Bell, M.Ed.
High School Speech,
Debate, & Competitive Drama Coach
Mesquite, Texas

Ricardo Miller is on the cutting edge of Developing Children's Ministry Leaders; as well as parents. He has the leadership capabilities and the heart to lead the next generation to their next level of reaching the world's children for Christ, but he also has the insight and wisdom to know that parents are a key ingredient in reaching their children for Christ.

Sylvia White
Childcare Expert
Charleston, South Carolina

For many years, I admired the work and ministry of Pastor Ricardo Miller, even before I met him in person. Today, I am honored to see the fruit of Ricardo's 20 years of ministry and proven leadership, documented in this step-by-step guide "Parenting with a Purpose". This is a must read for Pastors, Children's Ministers, Church Workers and Volunteers. I believe this will be your best investment in THE NEXT GENERATION!

Bishop DJ Roker
Redemptive Life Church Int'l
Memphis, Tennessee

Ricardo Miller is the best Children's Evangelist I have ever met. He totally understands our Lord's command when, He said "suffer the children to come unto me and do not turn them away for the kingdom of God belongs to them." Sir Miller knows how to get any child to pay close attention and at the end, develop a heart for God. The formulas he prescribes will provoke this generation to invest into the next generation. These principles are creating a wave of purpose for the next generation here in Jamaica.

Bishop Mark S. Mclean
New Testament Church of God
Westmoreland, Jamaica

There is a paradigm shift in the methodology used to reach children in synergy with their parents today. In this book, Ricardo has expressed his contemporary leadership and teaching skills with the use of today's tested tools to make parents understand this new shift for purposeful parenting

Pastor Kikelomo Omooba
Annie's Place Child Development Initiative
Lagos, Nigeria

Ricardo Miller is the leader of a new generation of children's ministry development and leadership experts. He lives and breathes the strategies and tools he shares with hundreds of children's ministry leaders. Ricardo's content is rich and practical, and his style is dynamic and engaging! If you want to see real change in your life, or the life of your children's ministry, connect with Ricardo Miller.

Minister Jason Basden
Nassau, Bahamas

Edwards Brothers Malloy
Thorofare, NJ USA
April 20, 2016